FRONTLINE FAMILIES

THE CIVIL WAR

Frontline Soldiers and Their Families

Sara Howell

Gareth Stevens
PUBLISHING

Please visit our website, **www.garethstevens.com**. For a free color catalog of all our high-quality books, call toll free 1-800-542-2595 or fax 1-877-542-2596.

Library of Congress Cataloging-in-Publication Data
Howell, Sara.
The Civil War: frontline soldiers and their families / by Sara Howell.
p. cm. — (Frontline families)
Includes index.
ISBN 978-1-4824-3057-8 (pbk.)
ISBN 978-1-4824-3060-8 (6 pack)
ISBN 978-1-4824-3058-5 (library binding)
1. United States — History — Civil War, 1861-1865 — Juvenile literature.
2. United States — History — Civil War, 1861 - 1865 — Social aspects — Juvenile literature.
I. Howell, Sara. II. Title.
E468.H69 2016
973.7—d23

First Edition

Published in 2016 by
Gareth Stevens Publishing
111 East 14th Street, Suite 349
New York, NY 10003

© 2016 Gareth Stevens Publishing

Produced by Calcium
Editors for Calcium: Sarah Eason and Rachel Warren Chadd
Designers: Paul Myerscough and Jessica Moon
Picture researcher: Susannah Jayes

Picture credits: Cover: Wikimedia Commons: Library of Congress/Kurz & Allison; Inside: Dreamstime: Jesse Molnau 14; Shutterstock: American Spirit 7r, 35, 36, Donna Beeler 19, 26, 27, Boris15 45br, Boykov 15tr, Steve Estvanik 17, 21r, Jose Gil 23l, 31l, Rainer Lesniewski 12, Karyl Miller 5r, I. Pilon 6, 29, Nicolas Raymond 44; Wikimedia Commons: 16, 34br, 37r, 38, Bowdoin College Museum of Art 8, Burns Archive 39l, Google Cultural Institute 28, Harper's Weekly 41tr, Heritage Auctions 13, Kansas State Board of Agriculture 9, Library of Congress 7tl, 21tr, 25, 33tl, 33b, 39tr, Library of Congress/Kurz & Allison 1, Jud McCranie 34tr, NARA 40, 43, Thure de Thulstrup 10, Treadwell & Peaslee 31r, U.S. Army 42, U.S. Naval Historical Center 5t, 15l, U.S. Post Office 37tl, United States Sanitary Commission 22–23, White House/Pete Souza 45l.

Printed in the United States of America
CPSIA compliance information: Batch #CS15GS: For further information contact Gareth Stevens, New York, New York at 1-800-542-2595.

CONTENTS

Chapter 1 A Country Divided   4

Chapter 2 War Breaks Out!   12

Chapter 3 Women of the War   18

Chapter 4 Children and Families   24

Chapter 5 The End of the War   32

Chapter 6 A Changed Nation   38

Glossary   46

For More Information   47

Index   48

A COUNTRY DIVIDED

For as long as humans have lived together in groups, there have been wars. People go to war for many reasons—fighting, for instance, over religion, natural resources, or ideas of how a government should be run. Many wars are fought between two or more countries. When two sides within the same country are fighting against each other, it is called civil war.

The American Civil War

Just over 150 years ago, the United States fought its own civil war. The Civil War was fought between the Confederate army of the South and the Union army of the North. Though many issues of the time divided Southern and Northern states, one of the most important was the issue of slavery. Nearly 4 million black people lived as slaves in the United States before the start of the war. Slave labor was an important part of the South's economy. However, many people, especially those in the Northern states, felt that slavery should not be allowed.

The Civil War began in 1861 when a group of Southern states voted to secede, or separate, from the United States of America. They believed that US president Abraham Lincoln intended to end slavery. Together, these Southern states formed the Confederate States of America. Over the next four years, war raged between the

Here, men in Civil War uniform reenact the Battle of Gettysburg to mark its 150th anniversary.

These Union soldiers stand near a cannon aboard the USS *Wissahickon* in 1863.

Confederate and Union armies. It is now believed that as many as 851,000 Americans may have died in the Civil War. Many were killed in battle, but far more died as a result of disease and poor medical treatment. Even today, the war remains the bloodiest in US history.

Families Left Behind

When we think about war, we often think of the soldiers who fight. However, many of those most affected are the families left behind. This was certainly the case during the Civil War. Women and children on both sides of the conflict faced many hardships, but they did whatever they could to help the war effort and support their fathers, brothers, husbands, and sons on the battlefield.

LIFE BEFORE THE WAR

Before the Civil War, life in Northern states was very different from life in the South. The economy in the North was based more on industry and manufacturing. The Southern economy focused largely on agriculture, or farming. Northerners and Southerners also held some very different political ideas.

Life in the South

Plantations—large crop-growing farms—were at the heart of the Southern economy. The warm weather and fertile soil in the South created perfect conditions for growing important cash crops, such as cotton and tobacco. Many Southern families, especially those with smaller farms, did not own any slaves at all. However, large plantations depended on slave labor; by 1860, there were nearly as many blacks in the South as whites.

Primary Source: What Does It Tell Us?

This advertisement for the sale of slaves appeared in a Virginia newspaper in the 1850s. It is placed right above an advertisement for the sale of property. What does that tell you about the way people of the time viewed slaves?

have lived in a drug store for several years. Use this as you think proper. Very truly, H. H. GEISIGER.
To Messrs. ROVE & Co.
ap14

PUBLIC SALE OF NEGROES.—Under the authority of a decree of the Circuit Court of Albemarle county, pronounced in the case of Michie's administrator and others, on the 8th day of October, 1855, I will offer for sale, at public auction, on MONDAY, the 5th day of May next, being Albemarle Court day, if a suitable day, if not, on the next suitable day thereafter, at the Court House of Albemarle county, *Five Negroes*, of whom the late David Tichis died possessed, consisting of a Negro Woman, twenty years of age and child two years old, a woman fifty-five years old, a negro man twenty-five years old, who has been working at the slating business, and a negro man twenty-two years old, a blacksmith.—The above lot of negroes is equal to any that has ever been offered in this market.

TERMS OF SALE—Five months credit, negotiable notes with approved endorsers, with the interest added.
ap24—ctds
GEO. DARR, Commissioner.

VALUABLE PROPERTY FOR SALE !—The subscriber, wishing to remove to a more Southern climate, offers for sale, his very desirable property. It is situated in one of the

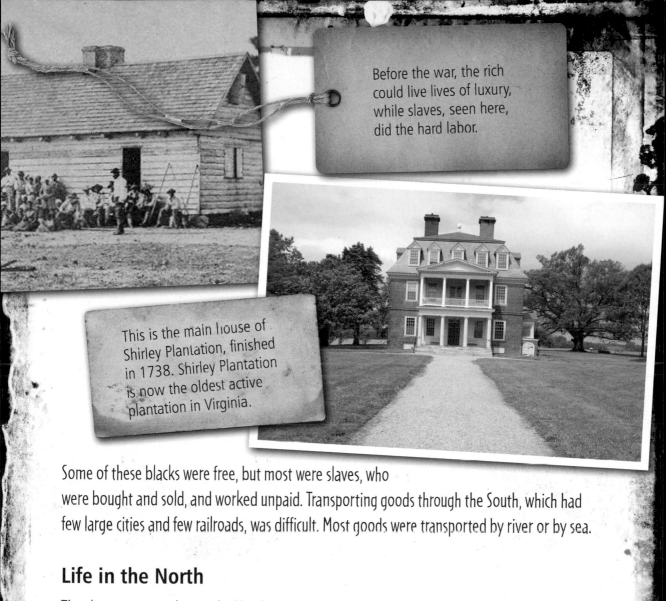

Before the war, the rich could live lives of luxury, while slaves, seen here, did the hard labor.

This is the main house of Shirley Plantation, finished in 1738. Shirley Plantation is now the oldest active plantation in Virginia.

Some of these blacks were free, but most were slaves, who were bought and sold, and worked unpaid. Transporting goods through the South, which had few large cities and few railroads, was difficult. Most goods were transported by river or by sea.

Life in the North

The climate, or weather, in the Northern states was not suited to large plantations. However, the region did have many natural resources, such as coal. Because of this, industry and the manufacturing of goods began to play a larger role in the economy. Factories were built, and towns grew into large urban centers. By 1860, a quarter of all Northerners lived in large cities. There was little need for slave labor, and immigrants from Europe did much of the lower-paid work. Northerners often had professional careers in business, engineering, and medicine. Children in the North were also more likely to go to school than those in the South.

CAUSES AND CONFLICTS

At the start of the Civil War, the United States had been an independent country for less than 100 years. As the country expanded its borders and grew to include new territories, its citizens found there was much on which they did not agree. Slavery was one of those issues.

Seeking Compromise

The structure of the US government was designed to ensure that each citizen was represented fairly. The number of representatives each state has in the House of Representatives is based on its population, and each state has two representatives in the Senate. As more territories became US states in the 1800s, people feared that either those who supported slavery or those who opposed it would gain too much power in the

Harriet Beecher Stowe was the author of *Uncle Tom's Cabin*, published in 1852. The book encouraged many to make a stand against slavery.

Primary Source: What Does It Tell Us?

This poster from 1855 was created by those who opposed slavery in Kansas. They are protesting a law that made it illegal for a person to speak out against slavery. The freedom of speech, or the right to speak and disagree with the government, is protected by the First Amendment to the US Constitution. Why would freedom of speech have been an important right for people at the time?

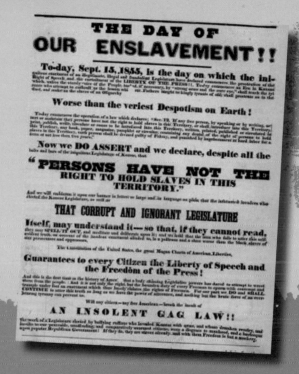

government. Before 1820, there were equal numbers of slave states, in which slavery was legal, and free states, where it was not. To maintain this balance, the Missouri Compromise of 1820 allowed Missouri to enter the United States as a slave state if Maine was allowed to enter as a free state; this helped to calm the issue for a while.

Bleeding Kansas

The balance of free states and slave states largely held until 1854, when the Kansas-Nebraska Act repealed (canceled) the Missouri Compromise. The Act allowed settlers of the new territories of Kansas and Nebraska to decide by vote whether slavery would be legal. Many people were angry, and violence erupted in the Kansas Territory between those who favored slavery and those who were against it. The violent conflicts, which took place over several years, are often called "Bleeding Kansas."

The Civil War lasted for four violent years. However, both the causes leading up to war and its effects afterward spanned decades. Here are a few of the important dates and events.

1850

September 18: The Fugitive Slave Act is passed by Congress, requiring all escaped slaves to be returned to their owners, even if they had reached free states. The law also required citizens in free states to cooperate.

1854

May 30: The Kansas-Nebraska Act, allowing settlers in new territories to vote freely on the slavery issue, is signed into law.

1860

November 6: Abraham Lincoln is elected president of the United States.

December 20: South Carolina officially secedes from the Union—within three months, six more states will secede.

Confederate and Union forces clash in the Battle of Antietam in 1862, where thousands died.

1861

January 29: Kansas is admitted to the United States as a free state.

February 8-9: The Confederate States of America is formed. Jefferson Davis is elected to serve as president.

March 4: Abraham Lincoln is inaugurated (formally confirmed) as US president.

April 15: President Lincoln calls for 75,000 volunteers to enlist in the Union army for three months.

April 17: The state of Virginia votes to secede from the Union—the eighth state to do so.

May 24: The Union army captures Alexandria, Virginia.

July 21: The First Battle of Bull Run, the first major battle of the war, is a victory for the Confederates.

1862

February 6: The Union army captures Fort Henry, Tennessee, opening the state for a Union advance.

March 8–9: The Battle of the Ironclads, in which the Confederate USS *Virginia* destroys two of the Union's wooden ships and fights to a draw with the Union's ironclad, the USS *Monitor*.

April 6–7: The Battle of Shiloh is fought. It is a Union victory, though both sides suffer huge losses.

August 28–30: The Second Battle of Bull Run, also named the Second Battle of Manassas, is fought, resulting in a Confederate victory.

September 17: The Battle of Antietam is fought. The inconclusive battle is the first to take place in Union territory. It remains the bloodiest single-day battle in US history.

December 11–15: The Battle of Fredericksburg is a Confederate victory with heavy Union losses.

1863

January 1: Abraham Lincoln issues the Emancipation Proclamation, freeing slaves in Southern territories.

July 1–3: The Battle of Gettysburg is fought, with the largest number of casualties of any Civil War battle. It is a Union victory.

July 13–16: Riots to protest the draft are held in New York City.

November 19: Abraham Lincoln delivers the Gettysburg Address.

1864

June 28: Abraham Lincoln repeals the fugitive slave laws.

September 2: Union commander General William T. Sherman captures the city of Atlanta.

November 8: Abraham Lincoln is reelected as US president.

1865

January 31: The US Congress passes the Thirteenth Amendment, abolishing slavery.

April 9: Robert E. Lee, commander of the Confederate Army of Northern Virginia, surrenders (gives up) to Union commander Ulysses S. Grant.

April 14: Abraham Lincoln is shot by John Wilkes Booth in Washington, D.C. He dies the next day.

June 2: The Confederate port of Galveston, Texas, finally surrenders, ending the war.

CHAPTER 2

WAR BREAKS OUT!

In November 1860, Abraham Lincoln was elected as the US president. Lincoln and his political party, the Republicans, opposed slavery and its expansion into new US territories. Lincoln's victory was the last straw for many Southerners.

Formation of the Confederacy

Just over a month after Abraham Lincoln won the 1860 presidential election, South Carolina voted to secede from the United States. Before Lincoln was inaugurated and took office in March 1861, six more states—Texas, Florida, Alabama, Mississippi, Georgia, and Louisiana—had broken away. Together with South Carolina, the seven states formed the Confederate States of America.

This map shows Union states and Confederacy states, and also US territories that were not yet states.

Union states without slavery
Union States with slavery
Confederate States
Territories

In February 1861, a meeting called the Peace Conference of 1861 was held in Washington, D.C. The goal of the meeting was to preserve the Union and reach a compromise on the slavery issue. The meeting, however, was unsuccessful, and its suggested compromises made neither side happy.

War Begins

By April 1861, tensions were rising between the Union and the newly formed Confederacy, as the Confederate States were also known. On April 12, Union ships attempted to resupply Union troops at Fort Sumter, in Charleston Harbor, South Carolina. Confederate forces fired on the Union troops, who eventually surrendered. Though the Battle of Fort Sumter did not result in any casualties, it is considered the start of the Civil War. The day after the battle, April 15, Abraham Lincoln called for 75,000 volunteers to join the Union army. Within a month, four more states—Virginia, Arkansas, Tennessee, and North Carolina—had seceded and joined the Confederacy.

Primary Source: What Does It Tell Us?

This broadside, printed on December 20, 1860, announces the secession of South Carolina from the United States. It was the first state to secede. Citizens who saw this bold announcement were probably unsure of what would happen next. Many families did not own slaves. If you belonged to one of those families, how do you think you might have felt about secession?

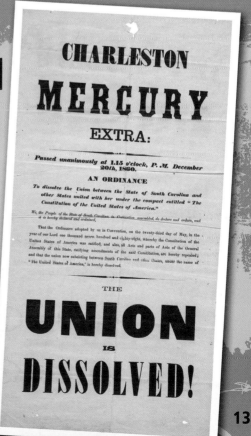

13

WEAPONS AND WARFARE

To our eyes, the Civil War might seem much like an ancient war. Soldiers rode into battlefields on horses, rather than in armored tanks. They fought with muskets and swords—not machine guns and guided missiles. However, many people actually consider the Civil War to be the first modern war, because of the roles that industry, transportation, and telecommunications played.

Weapons of War

Civil War soldiers used many different types of weapons on the battlefield. These included knives, swords, and bayonets, which are rifles with swords or knives attached to the ends. They also used many types of firearms, such as muskets, which needed to be reloaded after each shot. One type—named rifled muskets—used a grooved barrel that caused the bullet to spin as it left the barrel, which helped improve the accuracy of each shot. As the war went on, repeating firearms became more common. These guns, such as the Spencer rifles and Henry rifles, could fire several shots before being reloaded.

This type of revolver was used during the Civil War. Handguns were used most often by officers.

Men reenacting a Civil War battle load and fire a cannon similar to those that Union and Confederate forces used.

In 1864, the Confederates used a submarine, the CSS H. L. Hunley, to sink the Union's USS Housatonic.

Cannons were also very important during the Civil War. Artillery, such as the 6-pounder gun, the 12-pounder Howitzer, and the 1857 model 12-pounder—commonly called the "Napoleon"—were used to fire at enemies, both those in the open battlefield and those behind fortifications. The names referred to the size of the shots fired. Each cannon was a heavy piece of equipment and was often pulled by horses.

Air and Sea

Naval weapons also played a role during the war. After the battle between two ironclad ships, the USS *Virginia* and the USS *Monitor* on March 9, 1862, ships cased in iron or steel would replace the widely used wooden ships. Airplanes would not be developed for another 40 years, but Civil War forces found another way to use the skies. Hot-air balloons were sent up, primarily by the Union, to gather information about battle sites and the movement of enemy troops. Some could even send messages by telegraph to the ground.

FAMILIES DIVIDED

The Civil War is often called the war in which "brother fought against brother." While the country as a whole was divided over the issues of slavery and the rights of states, many families were divided as well.

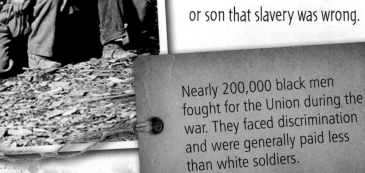

Conflicting Loyalties

In the Civil War era, just as today, families did not always agree on important issues. One family member's loyalty might be to the United States, while another's was to their home state, even when that state decided to secede. Parents might believe that owning slaves was their right and necessary for their economic survival, while the writings of abolitionists might have convinced their daughter or son that slavery was wrong.

Nearly 200,000 black men fought for the Union during the war. They faced discrimination and were generally paid less than white soldiers.

Primary Source: What Does It Tell Us?

John Fee was a Methodist minister from Kentucky. His father was a wealthy farmer who kept many slaves. In Fee's diary, he describes the arguments he had with his father about slavery, and how he tried to free one of his father's slaves, named Julett. What do you think Fee's account tells us about divided opinions over slavery in Southern families?

"My mother was displeased, -- did not want to spare the woman from certain work for which she was fitted. My father came to me and requested that I cancel the contract and give up the bill of sale. I said to him, 'Here is my horse, and I have a house and lot in Lewis County; I will give them to you if you so desire; but to sell a human being I may not.' He became very angry and went to the freed woman and said to her, 'When you leave this house never put your foot on my farm again....'"

At the time of the Civil War, women did not yet have the right to vote in state or national elections, but many were strongminded enough to form their own opinions about political matters, which could be very different from the views of their husbands.

Families Torn Apart

During the Civil War, these political disagreements could tear families apart. Many fathers, sons, and husbands left their homes to fight in the war—even though the rest of their family did not support their decision. Brutus Clay was a member of the Kentucky House of Representatives who supported the Union. Later in the war he served in Congress in Washington, D.C. However, in 1861, his son Ezekiel Field Clay left home in the middle of the night to join the Confederate army.

This man is dressed as a Confederate soldier. In the real war, some families had members on both sides.

CHAPTER 3

WOMEN OF THE WAR

The Civil War had a huge effect on family life. As men went off to war, women were forced to take on new roles at home to ensure their families' survival. Some women had the skills necessary to do so, while others were unprepared for the harsh realities of war.

A Woman's Role

In most families at the time of the Civil War, both in the North and in the South, the men were the primary breadwinners. This meant that they were the ones who worked outside the home to earn money, or that they did much of the manual labor on the family farm. The older sons in a family also worked and often contributed much of their earnings to their family. Most women did not work outside the home. Instead, they took care of the children and ran the household, which included work such as cooking and cleaning.

Changing Lives

When the Civil War began, husbands and older sons began leaving home by the thousands to go off to battle. This left many families without any source of income or way to run their farm. Women throughout the North and South had to take on new responsibilities, many of which they were neither trained nor prepared for. Young girls and women at the time were expected to be refined and cultured, but for the most part, had not been taught the many important skills necessary for daily survival.

This 1865 photo shows a young mother and her child. Like many women, she would have had to care for her family alone.

Now, some took on their husbands' roles in running businesses. Many began running and working their family farms, performing difficult physical tasks such as plowing fields and harvesting crops. For women used to hard labor, generally those from poorer families, this new work and responsibility was less of a challenge. However, for many middle-class women—particularly those in the South who were left to run plantations and manage slaves—life was very different. Yet, most of these women found the strength to do what needed to be done.

Women were not allowed to join either the Union or Confederate armies. However, many women felt it was their duty to help in any way they could to support the war effort. One way that they could do that was by volunteering as nurses on the battlefield and in hospitals. With thousands of men killed and wounded, and few doctors available, much of the care for injured soldiers fell to these women.

Civil War Medicine

Medical care at the time of the Civil War was very different from what it is today. There were no antibiotics to treat infections. Doctors were only just beginning to understand the existence of germs, and the importance of clean and sanitary conditions. Of the estimated 752,000–851,000 men who died during the Civil War, about two-thirds of them did not die directly from enemy fire, but from infections and diseases, such as tuberculosis, dysentery, measles, and typhoid fever.

Primary Source: What Does It Tell Us?

These are the words of a nurse named Julia Susan Wheelock. Wheelock went to Washington, D.C., in 1862, looking for her brother, who she learned had been killed. She worked in hospitals in the area for the rest of the war. What do you think it would have been like to care for enemy soldiers, especially after losing a family member?

"Many of these were Rebels. I could not pass them by neglected. Though enemies, they were nevertheless helpless, suffering human beings."

Disease spread quickly through war camps because of the dirty conditions and poor sanitation.

When injured soldiers were taken to makeshift hospitals, they did not fare much better than in the camps. Early in the war, hospitals had little organization. They were crowded, with more wounded men than they could handle. A hospital might be nothing more than tents outside, with wounded men lying on blankets on the ground.

Dorothea Dix, seen here, set guidelines for nurses—they had to be plain-looking and aged between 35 and 50.

Volunteer nurses were often from the North, but they cared for both Union and Confederate soldiers.

The Role of Nurses

It was into these conditions that thousands of women, many from the North, volunteered to become nurses. Nurses dressed wounds and assisted doctors with surgeries, including amputations. They spent time with the wounded, cheering their spirits, praying with them, and even helping them write letters home to their families. One of the most famous nurses of the war was Clara Barton, who was often called the "Angel of the Battlefield." After the war, she would go on to found the American Red Cross.

RELIEF EFFORTS

The women who left home to become Civil War nurses were generally unmarried, educated, and from middle-class families. Not all women were able to leave home to do their part to support the war but, throughout the North and South, women found many other ways to contribute to the war effort.

Gathering Supplies

One of the most important services that women could offer was to help provide essential supplies. These could include anything from blankets and socks to bandages and food. Amid the uncertainty of wartime, many women channeled their energies into collecting food or medical supplies for the soldiers. Making clothes for their husbands, sons, and brothers also gave them a sense of purpose. Coming together at events such as local sewing bees had a further benefit—women were able to connect with others who were suffering the same hardships and anxieties that they were.

Organized War Efforts

Some women extended their relief efforts and worked with organizations such as the United States Sanitary Commission, which operated across the North. The agency was created to support sick and wounded soldiers, and to promote clean and healthy conditions in Union army camps. Thousands of volunteers, many of whom were women, ran kitchens in army camps, oversaw soldiers' homes, and sewed uniforms. The Commission also organized Sanitary Fairs, which included parades, speakers, and art exhibitions, to raise money for the Union cause. Between 1861 and 1866, the Commission raised around $25 million in funds and donated supplies.

The US Sanitary Commission established this Soldiers' Home at Camp Nelson, in Kentucky.

Women on the Battlefield

Not all women were content to support the war effort from the sidelines. Though women were not allowed to join either the Union or Confederate armies, there are hundreds of known cases where women posed as men to join the army. Some, such as Lizzie Compton, were discovered by doctors after being wounded in battle. Others, such as Jennie Hodgers, went through the entire war without being found out. Some were only discovered when they gave birth in the army camp!

In uniform, disguised as male soldiers, women often looked much like the young men they fought beside.

Primary Source: What Does It Tell Us?

The discovery of women soldiers on the battlefield unnerved many male soldiers. In a letter home, Colonel Elijah H. C. Cavins of the 14th Indiana division asked his wife the question shown here. What do his mocking words tell us about how society at the time viewed women?

"What use have we for women, if soldiers in the army can give birth to children?"

CHAPTER 4

CHILDREN AND FAMILIES

Women were not the only ones affected by a changed home life during the Civil War. Millions of children said goodbye to their fathers and older brothers, knowing they might never see them again. Families worked hard to stay as connected as they could to the soldiers who had left to fight. Writing letters was one way to keep in touch. Some families were even able to visit their fathers and brothers in army camps!

Letters of Love

Today we are able to keep in touch with friends and families in many ways, including via telephone calls, texts, emails, and even video chats. During the Civil War, however, none of this technology existed. The only way for families to communicate with soldiers in distant camps was by writing letters. The letters written to soldiers often told of daily life at home. Families also discussed major events of the war. The letters that soldiers wrote back describe battles and life in the army camps.

Families were happy to receive letters from relatives and friends in the armies, and to know they were still alive and well. Soldiers were equally anxious to receive letters that showed their loved ones were thinking of them, and that they had not been forgotten.

Primary Source: What Does It Tell Us?

This is part of a letter written by a Union soldier named Sullivan Ballou. Ballou was killed during the First Battle of Bull Run. The letter to his wife was found after his death. Do you think other soldiers had similar thoughts? How do you think his wife and family would have felt reading it?

July the 14th, 1861
Washington D.C.

My very dear Sarah:

The memories of the blissful moments I have spent with you come creeping over me, and I feel most gratified to God and to you that I have enjoyed them so long. And hard it is for me to give them up and burn to ashes the hopes of future years, when God willing, we might still have lived and loved together and seen our sons grow up to honorable manhood around us. I have, I know, but few and small claims upon Divine Providence, but something whispers to me—perhaps it is the wafted prayer of my little Edgar—that I shall return to my loved ones unharmed. If I do not, my dear Sarah, never forget how much I love you, and when my last breath escapes me on the battlefield, it will whisper your name.

As important as these letters were for people at the time, they are important for us today, too. The letters that have survived give us a glimpse of what life was like during the war, what people thought about major events, and what they believed they were fighting for.

Here, Abraham Lincoln sits with his youngest son, Tad. Tad was just 12 years old when his father was assassinated.

THE LIVES OF CHILDREN

In some ways, the lives of children before the Civil War were very different from what most US children experience now. There were no televisions or video games to entertain them, and they often had many chores and responsibilities at home. In other ways, children of the 1800s were much like kids today. They enjoyed playing games, and spending time outdoors and with their families.

Childhood Before the War

In the years before the Civil War, families often had many children. The more children there were in a family, the more hands there were to help. A large family was especially important for families who farmed. Both parents and children generally woke before the sun was up and got to work. Children milked cows, gathered eggs from the henhouse, and got water from the well. Older sons could help their father plow fields, while daughters often helped their mother prepare food for the day and wash clothes. Many children also went to school, while others studied at home. They made time for play, too, and would enjoy fishing, hunting, and having fun with siblings and friends.

Comfortable living vanished in the war. Many children, especially in the South, saw their homes turned into field hospitals and command posts.

Primary Source: What Does It Tell Us?

Emma LeConte was 17 years old when she wrote these words in her diary. She had just witnessed the burning of her hometown—Columbia, South Carolina. What do you think she means by the "wicked feelings" she describes? How do you think children like her would have felt about those on the opposing side?

"As to the condition of the country and our unhappy state as a people, it would seem better not to think of that, still less to write of it. It makes me miserable and intensifies the wicked feelings I have too much anyway."

Losing a husband or father in the war could devastate a family, both emotionally and financially.

New Roles and Responsibilities

Before the Civil War, life for many families was difficult. When the war began, however, conditions for many families became even harder. With their fathers and older brothers away fighting, children often took on new responsibilities as their families learned to adjust to life during war. Children helped their mothers run farms, performing difficult tasks such as harvesting crops and butchering animals. Many also had to take care of younger siblings while their mothers worked.

Some children had to leave school so they could provide more help at home. For those who were lucky enough to stay in school, lessons often focused on the war, promoting one or the other side's cause, and encouraging patriotism and loyalty.

HARDSHIP IN THE SOUTH

Many Northerners faced hardships during the Civil War, such as separation from their husbands, sons, and brothers, and not knowing if their loved ones would ever return. However, Southerners suffered all this and then some. For them, every aspect of life was affected by war, as many of the battles were taking place in their own backyards!

Primary Source: What Does It Tell Us?

This painting by Eastman Johnson is named *A Ride for Liberty—The Fugitive Slaves*. It was painted in 1862. In it, a slave family, made up of a father, mother, and two young children, escape on horseback toward Union troops. While the father looks forward, the mother looks behind her. What do you think each family member might have been feeling?

During the war, the price of goods in the South rose by 9,000 percent—Confederate money became worthless.

Witnesses to War

Most of the battles of the Civil War took place in the South. This meant that Southern families—more often than those in the North—were direct witnesses to the harsh realities of war. Many towns and cities in the South were destroyed, including Atlanta, Georgia. Some parts of Atlanta were destroyed by Confederate troops as they retreated, though most of the destruction was at the hands of occupying Union troops led by General William T. Sherman. When Sherman's troops had left, out of 3,600 homes and buildings around the city center, only 400 were still standing.

Worthless Money

As the war went on, the North was able to block many supplies from traveling through the South. This meant that items families needed, including food, became either very expensive or impossible to find. Confederate money became worthless, which made it even harder for families to buy the things they needed to survive. Many Southern families were close to starvation. What few food supplies and valuables they did have were often stolen by bands of Union—or even Confederate—troops, who were also hungry. Some families were forced to leave their homes.

CHILDREN ON THE BATTLEFIELD

Throughout the war, children were encouraged to support their soldiers in any way they could. For most, this meant raising money and collecting supplies. Some children took their support a step further, though, and actually joined the fight.

Boys at War

The Union army set the minimum age for soldiers at 18 years old. However, it is thought that around 100,000 Union soldiers were actually boys under the age of 15. The Confederate army did not set an age requirement. Of the total number of Civil War soldiers, it is thought that about 20 percent were under the age of 15. Young boys were generally able to join the Union and Confederate armies by lying about their age. As the war went on, the armies became increasingly desperate for more soldiers.

Primary Source: What Does It Tell Us?

The words here were written by Elisha Stockwell, who was 15 years old when he joined the Union army. Many boys joined the fighting because they were looking for adventure. Can you think of some other reasons why children would have wanted to join the war?

"I want to say, as we lay there and the shells were flying over us, my thoughts went back to my home, and I thought what a foolish boy I was to run away and get into such a mess as I was in. I would have been glad to have seen my father coming after me."

Recruiters–people who looked for new soldiers–often accepted boys into the army even if they suspected they were underage.

Boys also joined the army as musicians, drummer boys, messengers, and scouts. These were roles that should have kept them safe for the most part. However, in the middle of a battle, many boys had to fight to protect themselves and their fellow soldiers.

The Drummer Boy of Chickamauga

One of the most famous child soldiers of the war was a boy named Johnny Clem. He was only 10 years old when he joined the Union army as a drummer boy. At the Battle of Chickamauga, when a Confederate colonel demanded he surrender (give up), the boy, then 12, raised his musket and shot the officer. Johnny Clem became a hero, and continued to serve in the US army until he retired in 1915.

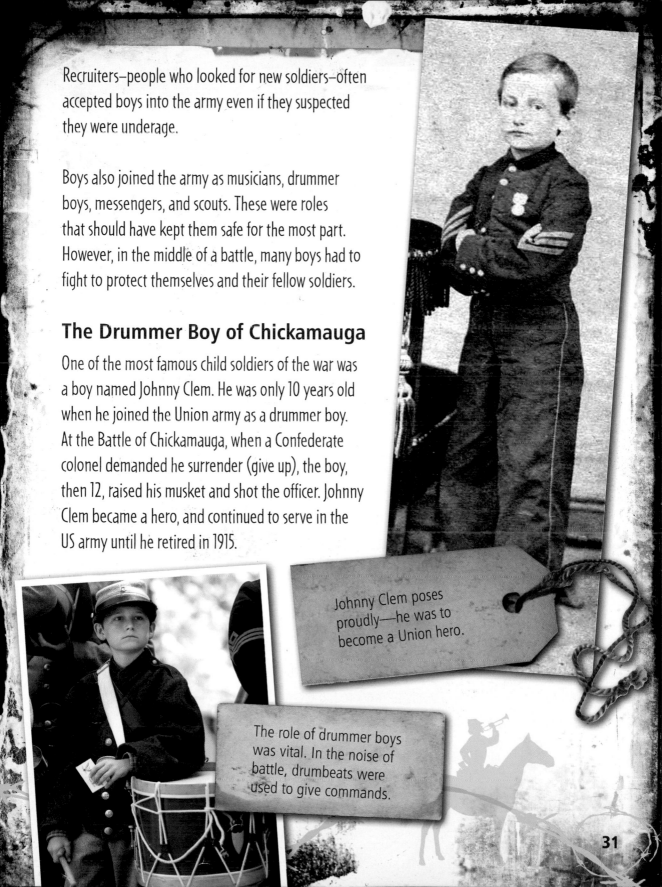

Johnny Clem poses proudly—he was to become a Union hero.

The role of drummer boys was vital. In the noise of battle, drumbeats were used to give commands.

CHAPTER 5

THE END OF THE WAR

After four long years of fighting, Confederate troops were worn down and spread thin. Northern resources had held out, while Southern resources had been heavily depleted. Hundreds of thousands of men on both sides of the conflict had been killed, and many more were injured. The fighting was nearly over, and though the Confederacy had won many battles, the Union would win the war.

The Battle of Appomattox Court House

On April 9, 1865, one of the last battles of the Civil War was fought in Virginia. Following the Union army's Siege of Petersburg, which had lasted for 10 months, General Robert E. Lee and the Army of Northern Virginia left the Confederate capital of Richmond. Lee hoped to move his soldiers back to North Carolina and meet up with other Confederate troops. However, Union forces cut off their retreat at the Appomattox Court House. The Confederate forces tried to break through, but they were surrounded. Lee sent a message to Union commander Ulysses S. Grant that he would like to meet to discuss surrender. On the afternoon of April 9, Lee officially surrendered to Grant. Within two months, nearly all Confederate troops had surrendered.

Lincoln Is Assassinated

With the surrender of Robert E. Lee's troops, spirits in the North were high. However, just a few days later, on April 14, President Abraham Lincoln was shot while attending a play in Washington, D.C. He would die early the next day. When an important person, such as a president, is killed it is called an assassination. The man who assassinated Abraham Lincoln was an actor named John Wilkes Booth. By killing the president, he and his conspirators hoped to revive the Confederacy. Booth was cornered and killed during capture on April 26. Vice President Andrew Johnson was sworn in as US president on April 15.

Abraham Lincoln is often considered one of the greatest US presidents.

The conspirators also planned—but failed—to kill the vice president and the secretary of state.

THE ASSASSINATION OF PRESIDENT LINCOLN,
AT FORD'S THEATRE WASHINGTON. D.C. APRIL 14TH 1865.

With the war over, there was hope that family life might go back to the way it had been. However, hundreds of thousands of men never went home. Women had become widows and children had lost their fathers. One out of every three households in the South had lost at least one family member.

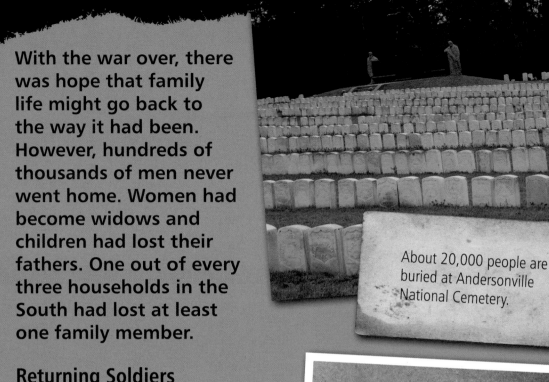

About 20,000 people are buried at Andersonville National Cemetery.

Returning Soldiers

Many army companies had been recruited from small towns and counties close together. When these companies were wiped out on the battlefield, it was devastating for their hometowns. Some towns and counties had lost almost their entire male population.

Alfred Stedman Hartwell was a lawyer who fought in the war. Like other returning war veterans, he had to make the difficult transition from soldier to ordinary citizen once more. Alfred managed to resume his career in law and went on to become a judge and a cabinet minister.

Secondary Source: What Does It Tell Us?

This photograph shows an exhibit at the Andersonville National Historic Site, in Georgia. Camp Sumter, also known as Andersonville Prison, was a Confederate prison built to hold captured Union soldiers. Over 14 months, it held about 45,000 Union soldiers. Conditions at the prison were awful, and nearly 13,000 prisoners died due to disease, malnutrition, and exposure to the elements. Using what we now know about germs and keeping clean, can you think of ways in which those in charge could have helped their prisoners stay healthy and disease-free?

Of the soldiers who did return home, many lived with the effects of the war for the rest of their days. Large numbers of men had had one or more limbs amputated, or cut off, to save their lives. This loss of limbs made manual labor nearly impossible for many. With the consequent loss of labor and income, many families fell into poverty.

Psychological Scars

For soldiers the aftereffects were not only physical. Many also suffered emotional and psychological problems after returning home. They often found it difficult to adjust back to their life at home after years on the battlefield and the horrors that they had seen. Psychological problems were not well understood at the time, and there was very little help available to those who were suffering.

During the four years of fighting, there was not often a lot of time to reflect on what had been lost. People were more concerned with everyday survival and the safety of their loved ones. However, once the war was over, many in the North and South worked to heal the divided country's wounds and to make sure that future generations would not forget their struggles.

Dealing with the Dead

By the war's end, it is now thought that at least 752,000 men—and possibly as many as 851,000—had died. That was between two and three percent of the entire US population at the time. In some of the major battles, thousands had died in a single day. In the middle of war, there was little time or manpower to deal with the huge number of bodies.

Secondary Source: What Does It Tell Us?

Some soldiers killed in battle were quickly buried near the battlefield by their fellow comrades. Many bodies, though, had to be simply left on the ground, exposed to the elements and unclaimed. Hundreds of thousands would never be identified, and their families would never know for sure what had happened to them, or where they had died. What effect do you think this had on the families of soldiers who never returned from battle?

These US postage stamps were issued in the 1960s to commemorate the 100th anniversary of several important Civil War battles.

National Cemeteries

Before the war, there were no national cemeteries. There were no procedures in place for identifying bodies, burying them, or notifying family members. The Civil War made Americans aware that these things were very much needed. Arlington National Cemetery, the most famous national cemetery today, was established in 1864. In 1867, two years after the end of fighting, Congress set up a program to rebury Union soldiers in 74 national cemeteries. The exclusion of Confederate soldiers upset many in the South.

Many Civil War monuments have been erected, such as this one to African American soldiers in Vicksburg National Military Park.

Memorial Day Origins

With thousands of the war's soldiers buried, families began gathering at graves and bringing flowers. This occasion was known as Decoration Day. In 1868, a former Union general named John Logan officially declared May 30 as a day to decorate the graves of fallen soldiers. Today, we celebrate this event as Memorial Day, on the last Monday in May.

A CHANGED NATION

With the Civil War over, the question facing the US government was how to reconcile the two sides of the conflict and bring the former Confederate states back into the Union. The time period beginning with the end of the war in 1865 and lasting until 1877 is known as the Reconstruction Era. During this time, the US government tried to "reconstruct" the South.

Bringing the South to the Union

Abraham Lincoln believed it would be best to bring the South back into the Union quickly and with as little conflict as possible. After Lincoln's assassination, President Andrew Johnson supported this plan. However, there were others in the government who believed that former Confederates should be punished for their rebellion. This group, called the "Radical Republicans," also wanted to give African Americans equal rights, including the right to vote in elections. The forceful group and Johnson could not agree.

After many conflicts with the Radical Republicans, Andrew Johnson was almost removed from office in 1868.

Primary Source: What Does It Tell Us?

This political cartoon from 1865 shows Andrew Johnson on the left and Abraham Lincoln on the right, attempting to repair the Union. Based on your reading, do you think the period after the war might have been different if Abraham Lincoln had lived?

THE "RAIL SPLITTER" AT WORK REPAIRING THE UNION.

However, the next president, Ulysses S. Grant, sided with the Radical Republicans. Congress removed many state governments in the South and put the US army in charge. New elections were held in which African Americans were allowed to vote and many former Confederate leaders were not. The policies angered Southerners. A group called the Ku Klux Klan began to carry out attacks against African Americans and whites who supported Reconstruction. Often through voter fraud and violence, groups of white Democrats took back state governments one by one.

Ending Reconstruction

After a controversial election in 1876, the Electoral Commission agreed to declare Republican Rutherford B. Hayes as president over Democrat Samuel Tilden. In exchange, Hayes was compelled to remove the last of the US troops in former Confederate states. This so-called Compromise of 1877 effectively ended Reconstruction.

Here, a crowd celebrates the Emancipation Proclamation of 1863—for some historians this marked the start of the Reconstruction Era.

RECONSTRUCTION AMENDMENTS

The Reconstruction Era is considered mostly a failure. Many of the actions of the US government in the South caused even more anger and resentment. However, some good came from the era in the form of the Reconstruction amendments—three amendments to the US Constitution relating to the rights and treatment of African Americans.

Adjusting the Constitution

The US government is designed so that laws and rules written into the Constitution are the most important, overruling those passed by the states. States cannot pass laws that go against the laws of the US Constitution. Therefore, the best way to enact a controversial law, such as the banning of slavery, was to make it an amendment, or change, to the Constitution. The former Confederate states were then forced to ratify, or approve, these amendments as a condition of once again having representation in the federal government.

Three Steps Toward Equality

The Thirteenth Amendment, ratified on December 6, 1865, abolished slavery within the United States. The Fourteenth Amendment gave citizenship to all people born or naturalized in the United States, including former slaves.

The Thirteenth Amendment, seen above, abolished slavery except as punishment for a crime.

The Fourteenth Amendment was ratified on July 9, 1868. Declaring African Americans citizens was an important step. In the 1857 Dred Scott case, the Supreme Court had ruled that neither free nor enslaved African Americans were citizens, and therefore had no right to sue for their freedom in federal court. The Fourteenth Amendment gave them that right.

The Fifteenth Amendment gave African American men the legal right to vote in elections   a right granted to all women only in 1920.

The Fifteenth Amendment–stating that the right of male citizens to vote could not be denied because of race or color–was the last of the Reconstruction amendments, ratified on February 3, 1870. All three Reconstruction amendments advanced equality, but did not solve the problems of racial injustice. It would be another 100 years before African Americans would experience a full sense of freedom and equal protection under the law.

Primary Source: What Does It Tell Us?

This is what the Fifteenth Amendment states. How do you think former slave-owning plantation farmers viewed the amendment? Why do you think it was so difficult for the federal government to make Southerners comply with it?

"The right of citizens of the United States to vote shall not be denied or abridged by the United States or by any State on account of race, color, or previous condition of servitude."

LEGACY OF THE CIVIL WAR

After the Reconstruction Era, Southern Democrats took control of the state governments of the former Confederate states. While they could not pass laws that went against the US Constitution, they found many ways around the laws. The rules that kept whites and blacks segregated and unequal for nearly 100 years are often known as the Jim Crow laws.

The Right to Vote

For a short time during Reconstruction, African American males had the right to vote in elections. However, once Southern Democrats regained control of state governments, they introduced laws that effectively prevented blacks from voting. For instance, literacy tests required African Americans to answer difficult–and sometimes nonsensical–questions before being allowed to vote, which most could not do. Poll taxes compelled people to pay a certain amount before being allowed to vote, which many poor people could not afford. Those who could not vote were also not allowed to serve on juries or hold public office.

In 1957, US soldiers were needed to escort nine African American students to class as Little Rock's Central High School was desegregated.

At the March on Washington for Jobs and Freedom in 1963, Martin Luther King Jr. gave his "I Have a Dream" speech in front of the Lincoln Memorial.

Separated by Law

African American children and families also suffered because of Jim Crow laws. Most areas of daily life, such as public schools, libraries, workplaces, restaurants, restrooms, and even drinking fountains, were segregated. This meant that blacks and whites had to use separate facilities. Under the law, the facilities were supposed to be "separate but equal." In practice, however, schools and other facilities for African Americans were underfunded and of lower quality.

The Civil Rights Movement

In the 1950s and 1960s, many people set out to change the culture of segregation and inequality for African Americans. Using nonviolent protests and civil disobedience, heroes of the movement—such as Rosa Parks and Martin Luther King, Jr.—put their lives and freedom on the line to effect change. The Civil Rights Act of 1964, signed by President Lyndon Johnson, made it illegal to discriminate against a person based on their race, color, sex, national origin, or religion. The act ended the segregation of public schools and public places, and any practices used to prevent people from voting.

The American Civil War remains the bloodiest war in US history. It had a huge influence over the country that we are today. We often focus on the soldiers who fought and died. However, it is important to remember that the war changed the lives of women, children, and families, both white and black, free and slave, as well.

Losses and Gains

The Civil War had a dramatic and lasting effect on our country. It took a long time to heal from the wounds and the hardship that the war inflicted, and some of that healing still continues in the generations that came after. For those who lived through the Civil War, life would never be the same. On both sides of the conflict, nearly every person suffered loss. Hundreds of thousands lost a husband, brother, father, or son. Many families lost their homes and possessions, too.

The Ulysses S. Grant Calvary Memorial stands at the base of Capitol Hill in Washington, D.C.

Secondary Source: What Does It Tell Us?

In this photo from 2010, President Barack Obama views the original Emancipation Proclamation. The document, signed by Abraham Lincoln in 1863, freed the slaves in Confederate states. President Obama is the first African American president of the United States. He was elected in 2008, less than 150 years after the end of the Civil War. What does this tell you about the changes in the United States since the Civil War? How do you think the United States might be different if the Civil War had not occurred?

For all the loss, however, much was gained as well. Slavery was abolished, and the North and South slowly came back together to form a stronger country—more united than ever. Throughout the twentieth century, African Americans made great gains in civil rights and equality. Once barred from voting, African Americans now serve in key government positions, and one man rose to the highest office of all—the presidency!

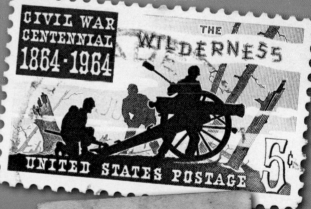

The Civil War continues to be remembered and commemorated, more than 150 years after it ended.

GLOSSARY

agriculture the science or practice of growing crops and raising livestock, or animals

amendment addition or change to a document, law, or set of laws, such as the Constitution

amputations surgical operation to cut off or remove limbs or parts of limbs

artillery cannons, large guns, or other weapons for firing over long distances

bayonets sharp knives attached to the front ends of rifles for use in close-range combat

casualties people who are injured or killed in an accident or a war

citizens people who are born in a country or legally permitted to live there and benefit from its rights and protection

compromise way of avoiding conflict by giving up something in order to reach agreement

economy wealth and resources of a country or region in terms of goods and services

Emancipation Proclamation official order, signed by Abraham Lincoln during the Civil War, that freed all slaves held in the South

fugitive someone who is running away from someone or something

infections illnesses caused by germs

ironclad ships ships covered with iron or steel to protect them from shot

muskets long-barreled firearms used before the invention of more efficient rifles

patriotism pride in one's country

plantation very large farm–usually in a hot region–where crops, such as cotton, are grown

political party organized group sharing similar beliefs about how a country should be run

representatives people elected to act or speak for the group who have chosen them

resources supplies of something necessary or valuable that can be used when required

retreat backing away from a fight or a dangerous, unpleasant, or difficult situation

sanitation use of measures, such as cleanliness, to prevent disease and protect public health

secede withdraw from a group or a country

telegraph machine used to send messages through wires using coded signals

US Constitution document adopted in 1788 that explains the different parts of the US government and the basic rights of citizens

FOR MORE INFORMATION

Books

Baumann, Susan K. *Black Civil War Soldiers: The 54th Massachusetts Regiment* (Jr. Graphic African American History). New York, NY: PowerKids Press, 2014.

Fitzgerald, Stephanie. *The Split History of the Civil War* (Perspectives Flip Books). North Mankato, MN: Compass Point Books, 2013.

Moss, Marissa. *Nurse, Soldier, Spy: The Story of Sarah Edmonds, A Civil War Hero*. New York, NY: Harry N. Abrams, 2011.

Thompson, Ben. *Guts & Glory: The American Civil War*. New York, NY: Little, Brown Books for Young Readers, 2014.

Websites

Discover when and where Civil War battles were fought at:
storymaps.esri.com/stories/civilwar

Find out more important Civil War facts at:
www.civilwar.org/education/history/10-facts-about-the-civil-war

Learn about Arlington Cemetery, its monuments, and notable graves at:
www.arlingtoncemetery.mil

Publisher's note to educators and parents: Our editors have carefully reviewed these websites to ensure that they are suitable for students. Many websites change frequently, however, and we cannot guarantee that a site's future contents will continue to meet our high standards of quality and educational value. Be advised that students should be closely supervised whenever they access the Internet.

INDEX

African Americans 16, 37, 38, 39, 40–43, 45
  see also slavery
amputations 21, 34, 35
Antietam, Battle of 10, 11
Appomattox Court House, Battle of 32
Arlington National Cemetery 37
assassination of Lincoln 33
Atlanta 11, 29

Barton, Clara 21
black soldiers 16, 37
Bleeding Kansas 9
blockades 29
Booth, John Wilkes 11, 33
boy soldiers 30–31
Bull Run, Battles of 10, 11, 25

causes of war 4, 8–9
children 7, 24, 26–27, 30–31
Civil Rights movement 43
Clem, Johnny 31
Confederate army 4, 5, 10–11, 17, 30, 32
Confederate states 4, 12, 13
Constitution 9, 40–41

Emancipation Proclamation 11, 39, 45

freedom of speech 9

Gettysburg, Battle of 5, 11
government, US 8–9, 38–39, 40, 42
Grant, Ulysses S. 11, 32, 39, 44

hot-air balloons 15

Jim Crow laws 42–43
Johnson, Andrew 33, 38, 39

Kansas-Nebraska Act 9, 10
Ku Klux Klan 39

Lee, Robert E. 11, 32
letter writing 24–25
Lincoln, Abraham 4, 10, 11, 12, 13, 25, 33, 38, 39, 45
loyalties, conflicting 16–17

medical care 5, 20–21, 22, 34, 35
Memorial Day 37
Missouri Compromise 9
monuments 37, 44
mortality figures 5, 36

national cemeteries 34, 37
naval battles 11, 15
Northern economy 6, 7
nurses 20–21, 22

Obama, Barack 45

plantations 6, 7, 19
prisons 35
psychological aftereffects 35

Radical Republicans 38, 39
Reconstruction Era 38–41

Sanitary Commission 22, 23
segregation 42–43
slavery 4, 6–7, 8, 9, 10, 11, 12, 13, 16, 17, 28, 40, 45
Southern economy 4, 6
Southern hardships 28–29
Stowe, Harriet Beecher 8
supplies 22, 29

Union army 4, 5, 10–11, 16, 30, 32, 35

voting rights 38, 39, 41, 42, 43

weapons 14–15
women 17, 18–23
women soldiers 23